Ache

by Ayn Asif

Writer's Pocket

First published by Writer's Pocket in 2023

email: publish@writerspocket.com

cover design by Pooja Wadiya

ISBN-13: 978-93-6083-889-8

www.writerspocket.com

CONTENTS

ACKNOWLEDGMENTS

This book is a culmination of my deepest thoughts over my high school years. So undoubtedly, my biggest supporters were my family.

My mom was ready at any time of the day to hear me spout my poems. Thank you, Umma.

My dad was a constant supporter of publishing my poems

My mamu was more enthusiastic about publishing them than I was and I'm really happy to have a mamu like him.

Finally, I'd like to say that this book is for all those who I've ever shared my poems with. It is my gesture of deep trust.

1. A delicate thing

Perhaps she was glass, a delicate thing,
A fragile soul, a heart that could sing.
But glass is only brittle until it breaks,
Then it's sharp, a shattered heart that makes.

Her eyes were like crystal, clear and bright,
A reflection of all the joy in sight.
But with one crack, they shattered and fell,
Leaving only shards of pain to tell.

Her voice was like a melody, sweet,
A gentle breeze that brought us to our feet.
But once it broke, it left a scar,
A painful reminder of what we are.

She was a flower, delicate and rare,
A beauty to behold, beyond compare.
But like all things fragile, she could fall,
And leave us with nothing but her call.

2. A facade my face puts on

Depression, a weight that I can't hide,
A heavy burden that I can't abide,
It drains my strength, it steals my cheer,
Leaves me feeling empty, year after year.

My face, a mask of happiness I wear,
A smile that hides the pain I bear,
My bright teeth and dimples, a facade,
A shield to protect the world from the shade.

But oh, the pain that I can't conceal,
The tears that I cry in secret, the reveal,
The emptiness that I can't disguise,
The loneliness that I can't surmise.

Depression, a beast that I can't tame,
A darkness that I can't proclaim,
It whispers lies, it steals my drive,
Leaves me searching for a light to survive.

But still, I put on a brave face,
A smile that hides the sorrow and disgrace,
My bright teeth and dimples, a facade,
A shield to protect the world from the shade.

3. A sacrifice for something unreal

I struggled and fought; I gave it my all.
But you kept on pushing, trying to make me fall.
I was killing me just to give us life.
As you stood by and watched, causing strife.

My lungs were burning, my vision blurred.
You never seemed to care or hear a word.
I was drowning, trying to save you from the deep
But you were only concerned with what you could keep.

I kept on fighting, even as I sank.
My heart was heavy, my mind in a blank
But through it all, I never lost sight.
Of trying to save you, with all my might.

In the end, I pulled us both to shore.
Despite the pain and wounds, I still wanted more.
For I knew that love was worth the fight
And I would do it all again, to save you that night.

4. A teenagers pov

Telling my parents my troubles,
Is like adding another bubble,
One that will burst and cause more strife,
And make me feel like I am running for my life.

They will worry, fret, and ask if I am okay,
And I will have to pretend that everything is okay,
When all I really want is to be left alone,
And deal with my problems on my own.

But deep down I know it is not the right way,
Keep my worries and fears at bay,
Sometimes I need someone to confide,
And let my emotions and thoughts collide.

So, I will take a deep breath and talk to my folks,
Even though it feels like my heart is being poked,
They are there to support and lend a hand,
Helping me move forward and understand.

5. Drowning

In the depths of deceit, where shadows roam,
My words, like waves, crash upon your shore,
With each falsehood told, my heart becomes stone,
Drowning in the sea of lies, forevermore.

Caught in a current of fabricated tales,
My soul, a shipwrecked vessel, lost at sea,
As I struggle to find truth's holy grail,
I sink deeper into this treacherous plea.

Oh, how I yearn to set my conscience free,
To swim away from this suffocating tide,
But the weight of my falsehoods drags at me,
An anchor, dragging my spirit down inside.

With every gasp for air, I choke in shame,
Knowing that I've betrayed your trust and love,
Yet still, I reach out, longing to reclaim,
That distant shore, where forgiveness may prove.

But as the waves crash over me, remorseful,
The burden of my sins pulls me low,
And though I strive to reach the shores remorseful,
I fear my lies have made redemption's door close.

For in the depths of my own deceit, I dwell,
A prisoner of falsehood, consumed by fears,
Yet still, I dream that one day I can tell,
The truth that releases me from these tears.

So, do forgive this drowning soul, I pray,
For in my lies, I'm lost and cannot find,
The way to shore, where truth lights up the way,
And I'll be free from the chains that bind.

But until that day, I'll drown in remorse,
And strive to find redemption in truth's embrace,
For its only then, with my lies staying course,
That I may find the shore where love finds its grace.

6. Happy people

The happiest people are those who give,
Not those who always aim to live.
For self alone, but selflessly
Forgive, forget, and spread their glee.

They love with hearts so full and bright,
And help to make things clear and right.
Their caring ways are truly rare,
For they give freely, without a care.

No grudges held, no bitterness,
Just smiles all around, and tenderness.
For they know that joy's contagious
And love's power is outrageous.

So be like those who have this gift,
And let your spirits soar and lift.
For you will find true happiness lies
In being a giver, not in taking tries.

7. Friends and reality

I'm tired of being lonely,
Even though I have many friends only,
They're just there to chit-chat and pass time,
Not realizing the loneliness that's mine.

I smile and laugh, playing my part,
Though inside me, I'm breaking apart.
I need a friend who'll hear my heart's cry,
And not just put up a superficial lie.

Don't get me wrong, my friends are great,
But there's a hole in my heart that won't abate.
I long for someone who'll understand,
And hold my hand, as we walk hand in hand.

I know I may seem cheerful and bright,
But that's just a facade, and not what's right.
I'm tired of being lonely, you see,
Please come and rescue me.

8. In the night, when I'm awake

In the dead of night, when all is still,
My heart sinks low, and my soul takes ill.
The darkness reigns, and the stars do hide,
Leaving naught but a blanket of sky wide.

The moon hides 'neath a veil of cloud,
And the world is quiet, devoid of crowds.
The darkness brings a sense of unease,
A feeling that all is not at peace.

But then, as I look up at the sky,
I see a glimmer of light, so high.
A star or two, shining bright and clear,
A beacon of hope, in all the fear.

Their twinkle reaches out, like a hand,
And guides my heart, through the dark land.
For in their light, I find a glow,
A sense that all will be well, somehow.

So, I wait, and watch, and pray,
For the dawn to come, and the night to fade away.
For in the light of a new day,
I know that all will be made right, in every way.

9. Stress: It hurts

I lost something I never had.
Yet it hurts, just as bad.
My life has been a constant mess,
A source of stress, it does regress,
I try to oversee all the strife,
But it is the weight that crushes life,

I wake up early, feeling numb,
With heaviness that makes me glum,
The thought of facing the day ahead,
Can fill my soul with pounding dread,

I try to smile, put on a face,
Hoping that my stress will erase,
But the strain is always there,
Mocking my attempts at peace to share,

Now I lay in my bed at night,
Lost in thoughts, no end in sight,
Praying for a break to ease my heart,
But it seems, even fate has played its part,

So, I continue, day by day,
Trying hard to find my way,
Holding on to hope and prayer,
Hoping that life's journey will be fair.

10. The heart and the head

A heart and a head, a wondrous pair,
In conversation, their thoughts so fair.
The heart, so full of love and grace,
The head, so full of wisdom and place.

The heart, it speaks of passion and fire,
The head, it speaks of reason and desire.
The heart, it yearns for love and light,
The head, it seeks for truth and might.

The heart, it dreams of sweet delight,
The head, it plans for the morning light.
The heart, it soars on wings of hope,
The head, it steadfast, a ship of scope.

The heart, it whispers secrets of the soul,
The head, it listens, and takes control.
The heart, it beats with love's sweet beat,
The head, it guides with reason's neat.

The heart and head, a perfect blend,
Together, their love will never end.
Their conversation, a beautiful song,
A harmony of love, all day long.

11. The memories of the past

In twilight's hush, where shadows dance and play,
Memories of the past, like ghosts, do come to stay.
Echoes of laughter, whispers of joy, so bright,
Fleeting moments, lost in the passage of time's flight.

The scent of roses, the taste of sweet delight,
Melodies of love, that once did take flight.
The warmth of sunshine, the sparkle of dew,
Faded now, but memories remain true.

The memories of past, they linger on,
A bittersweet longing, a wistful sigh, a song.
For though they fade, like autumn's leaves,
Their beauty remains, in our hearts, they breathe.

In twilight's hush, where shadows dance and play,
Memories of the past, like ghosts, do come to stay.

12. The mirror

In the glass, I saw a reflection so strange,
A face I didn't know, with features so bland.
The eyes that stared back, they didn't seem to belong,
To the body that held them, so weak and so wrong.

I searched for the me, that I once knew,
The one with the spark, and the heart that was true.
But all I found, was a shadow of doubt,
A reflection of fears, that I couldn't devout.

The lips that smiled, were painted with lies,
The hair that was styled, was a wicked disguise.
The skin that was smooth, was a mask of deceit,
A reflection of the insecurities, that I can't conceal.

I looked in the mirror, but I didn't see me,
The real me, the one that I'm meant to be.
I saw a stranger, a facade of perfection,
A reflection of the fears, that I can't correct.

13. Welcome to society

We welcome you here,
Society's open arms,
Hope you find solace.
Embrace the chaos,
Navigating this strange world,
Enjoy your sojourn.
In this grand hotel,
Where dreams and nightmares unite,
May joy light your way.
Seek connections deep,
Amidst the bustling city,
Find solace within.
Shadows may befall,
But remember, you are strong,
Face each trial head-on.
Embrace diversity,
For within our differences,
Lies true harmony.
Welcome, wanderer,
May your stay be filled with love,
In this tapestry.

14. When the society made us monsters

Why should I shut myself down?
When society never cared
About the pain we felt on the battleground
And the scars we all bear.

We fought for their ideals and their rights.
Risking everything, we had
Yet they still judge us with sight.
And ignore the wounds we have had.

A place in a world that does not understand.
The sacrifices we have made.
For every soldier, for every land
Our bravery should never fade.

So, I will not shut myself down.
I will stand up for what I believe.
In the battle for truth, I will wear the crown.
For the fighters who never received

The recognition they truly deserve.
And the respect they have earned.
For the sacrifices they had to serve
And the trauma they have learned.
We are not monsters, just warriors.
Who fought for a cause that was just?
So, let society hear our stories.
And let them know it is time to trust.

15. Rip Feelings

Nothing is more peaceful than having no interest in anyone,
No worries or distractions to get in the way of having fun.
I can wake up and have a quiet day with no plans,
Or spend time doing things I love, taking a leisurely stance.

No pressure to impress others or to meet their expectations,
I am content with myself and have no need for validations.
I do not have to keep up with trends or be a part of the crowd,
I can explore my own interests and never feel left out.

Some may find it odd or even think it is quite strange,
But for me, it is blissful, and there is nothing to exchange.
I appreciate the simplicity, the calmness and stillness too,
Having no interest in anyone is something I value and pursue.

16. Your apology?

My heart's in chaos, and my soul's on fire,
As I try to make sense of your words so dire,
I thought love was gentle, I thought love was kind,
But I cannot comprehend what's on your mind.

Your apologies fall like rain on my skin,
Yet the pain in my heart has never been,
More intense than it is, as I stand here alone,
Wondering where our love has gone.

Do you know the damage your words have done?
Can you hear the echoes of my heart undone?
I'm drowning in tears, suffocating in pain,
And all you can say is, "I'm sorry again."

But apologies don't mean a thing,
If your actions don't match what you're saying,
I need more than words, more than your lies,
I need you to show me or wave your goodbyes.

So, for now, I'll stand here, still, and numb,
And wait for the day when my heart will come,
Back to life, and find love once more,
But until then, I'll bear the pain you left me for.

17. Youth's way

In the midst of youth's wild rapture,
Lies a dream that's hard to capture,
Expectations soaring high,
The pressure rises, night by night.

The mind that seeks for earthly gains,
The heart that yearns for love's sweet strains,
The soul that longs for peace divine,
The three within, they never align.

A shattered dream, a broken heart,
It seems the world has played its part,
But in the depths of your despair,
Know that the Lord is always there.

Your parents may not see your pain,
Your friends may not share your strain,
Therapists claim they have a cure,
But only God's love can make it pure.

So, take His hand and trust His plan,
He'll guide you to the promised land,
Your teenage dream may be deferred,
But in His love, your heart's assured.

18. Living for myself

I am the master of my fate.
I am the captain of my soul.
I will not be confined by hate.
Or by society's rigid goal

My heart beats fiercely in my chest
Freedom and passion, my soul's quest
I will not conform to the norm.
I'll break the chains and stand up tall.

I choose my path, I forge ahead.
With strength, courage, and no dread
I am the artist of my life.
With my spirit as the guiding light

So, let society judge and sneer.
Their opinions won't cause me to fear.
I am a rebel, wild and free.
I live for me, not for society.

19. I would still pick up your call

Even in the stillness of night,
Your call would stir me to life,
For though it's been years,
My heart still holds you dear.

In the depth of my soul,
Your voice would make me whole,
For even time cannot erase,
The love that once took place.

For your voice is music to my ears,
And I've missed it so these past few years.
So even if it's just to hear you breathe,
I'll stay up with you, never wanting to leave.

Our time apart has been nothing but pain,
But speaking to you now, it feels like we're young again.
Time melted away, and love found a way,
To bring us back, where we should stay.

Though we may be worlds apart,
Your memory still holds my heart,
And I would answer your call,
After 3 years, and at 3 am, after all.

20. Blowing out the candles

I wish for hope, for strength and peace,
To make these heavy burdens cease.
But as I lie in bed at night,
I can't escape this endless plight.

My heart is heavy, my mind is numb,
And sadness lingers like a drum.
I try to push these thoughts away,
But they're here to stay, day after day.

I wonder when the sun will shine,
And when this darkness will decline.
But until then, I'll hold on tight,
To the little flicker of hope in sight.

I'll keep on going, one step at a time,
And pray that soon my heart will chime.
Till then, I'll talk to the stars above,
And keep blowing out candles with love.

21. Grateful

On mountain peaks and ocean shores,
I've seen the world in all its flaws.
I've climbed the heights, and swam the depths,
And felt the joy that nature begets.

I've heard the whisper of the breeze,
And felt the rustle of the leaves.
I've watched the stars, and felt their light,
Illuminate the darkest night.

For in the world around us, lies,
A splendour that can mesmerize.
A beauty that can touch the soul,
And make our spirits feel whole.

So let us take a moment, pause,
To see the wonders without cause.
And let the world, in all its might,
Remind us, we're alive tonight.

22. Parents

The weight of life bears down on him,
Yet still he stands with courage grim.
Through work and toil, he keeps his pace,
And strives to give his family grace.
His wife, a pillar at his side,
Nurtures their children, with love and pride.
She shares his pain, his every need,
A steadfast ally, a grace indeed.
Together they labour, day and night,
Building for the future, a family's light.
Saving every penny, with joy and glee,
Hoping for a life of prosperity.
Their days are hard, their nights are long,
Yet they keep going, steadfast and strong.
For they know that in their toil and strife,
Lies the hope for a better life.
They save their pennies, count each cent,
And pray their efforts aren't misspent.
For they dream of a life without the pain,
Where their children can flourish, without restrain.
For they know that soon, their children will grow,
And with their strength, a brighter future they'll sow.
Until that day, they labour with love,
Building a life, with blessings from above.

23. Clinging to something dead

In the depths of my heart,
There lies a bittersweet pain.
Memories of what once was,
Haunt me like a dark refrain.
I cling to what's no more,
Afraid to let it slip away.
Holding onto the memories,
That bring me joy each day.
But as time marches on,
I know I must learn to let go.
To free the chains that bind me,
And embrace the unknown.
For life is fleeting and fragile,
Each moment a precious gift.
So, I'll cherish every memory,
And let go of all that's left to sift.
Though it hurts to say goodbye,
And let the past fade into mist,
The beauty of today,
Is worth unwrapping in sweet bliss.
So, I'll release the sorrow,
And bask in the light of tomorrow.
For life is meant to be lived,
And not held hostage by dead and gone.

24. Jealousy

Jealousy is not my cup of tea,
I don't have time to waste my energy,
On petty emotions that only bring me down,
So, if you want to leave, I won't make a sound.

For I know my worth and I know my heart,
And if someone can't appreciate that, it's their loss,
I won't chase after anyone who wants to go,
I'll let them leave with grace, and my love will still flow.

So, you can have them, it's all good,
I'll move on and find someone who would,
Love me for who I am without any fear,
And cherish the moments we share, so dear.

For love should never be about possession,
It's about trust, honesty, and mutual affection,
And if we can't find that, we should let go,
And seek happiness elsewhere, in someone who knows.

25. Two different paths

Like two ships sailing in the sea,
Our paths crossed, inevitably.
We were not meant to be together,
But his touch made me feel tethered.

He whispered words that filled me with hope,
But I knew deep down, our love couldn't cope,
I tried to hold on, but it slipped away,
Leaving me in tears, left to pray.

Now I see that love is more than just a feeling,
It's the commitment and trust, that's the true meaning,
So, I let him go, with a heavy heart,
Hoping someday, we'll have a fresh start.

For now, I will cherish the memories we shared,
And the love we had, that once flared,
He may not be mine, but I'm glad he was once,
For he taught me love, the true essence.

For sometimes, belonging is just a feeling,
A fleeting joy that we hold onto, with no knowing.
And as our ships drifted apart,
I treasured the memories, still a part of my heart.

26. Acceptable

Your pain is visible, your hurt is clear,
And we all know that life isn't always fair,
But just because you're hurting, it's not okay,
To lash out or hurt others in the fray.

We all go through struggles, we all feel lows,
But it's important to control where your anger goes,
Don't take out your pain on those who care,
And don't let your hurt turn into a toxic snare.

It's okay to feel the pain and let yourself grieve,
But hurting others is not something you should conceive,
We all have bad days, we all feel weak,
But the real strength lies in how we choose to speak.

So, I urge you, dear friend, to find a way,
To deal with your pain, but in a positive way,
Don't let it control you or your behaviour,
For that's not the way to feel true treasure.

Instead, find ways to heal and move ahead,
And let go of your hurt, let your spirit spread,
You'll feel more whole, and your heart will mend,
And you'll realize, love can truly transcend.

27. Just stop

Amidst the hustle and bustle of life,
We forget to take a breather, just survive,
We're so consumed by phone screens and work,
That we forget to notice the beauty that lurks.

When was the last time you stopped and stared,
At the sunrise or sunset, so beautifully prepared?
Or looked up at the night sky, to see,
The glory of the moon and the stars so free?

Nature's art surrounds us every day,
But we're too busy to see it, to stop and play,
We rush and run, and our mind is cluttered,
Our spirit needs more, it needs to be nourished.

The gentle rustle of leaves, the soothing breeze,
The vibrant colours of flowers, and the melodies of bees,
All natural wonders, we miss in our haste,
Left in the background, but never to waste.

So, let's pause and take a deep breath,
And notice these gifts before their death,
Let's appreciate the beauty we're surrounded with,
And catch the moments that make our hearts lift.

For nature's magic is always there,
It's up to us to stop and stare,
To soak it in, and let it heal,
A moment of beauty, that's quite a feel.

28. Save it for someone who cares

Your feelings are valuable, they're true and real,
And they deserve to be acknowledged, to feel what you feel,
But don't waste them on people who don't bother,
Or who dismiss them, leaving you to suffer.

It's important to surround yourself with folks who care,
Who listen, understand, and are always there,
Those who cherish your heart, and your every thought,
And who lift you up when you feel caught.

Don't waste your emotions on those who aren't worth it,
Who only bring you down and cause you to hurt a bit,
Your feelings are a treasure, not to be wasted,
On those who don't appreciate them, or who seem pasted.

Find those who hear your voice, who validate you,
Who keep your secrets, and make you feel anew,
Your energy is valuable, it's a precious gift,
So, share it with those who uplift, who give you a lift.

And if someone's not worth your heart, it's not a loss,
You'll find people who care, and who'll help carry your cross,
Remember, you're worth it, and so are your feelings,
Cherish them, in safe spaces, with folks worth revealing.

29. Just a little push

I am sitting here today, feeling quite distressed,
My unhealthy habits have left me feeling quite oppressed,
I'm eating all the wrong foods and not getting enough sleep,
My thoughts are delusional, dark, and quite deep.

Sometimes it feels like the world is out to get me,
Like there's no point in trying, but oh how wrong I can be,
The negativity inside creates a downward spiral,
Pushing me deeper and deeper, the thoughts tend to pile.

But I cannot let my mind win, I'll fight this war,
I'll take small steps to improve my health for sure,
I'll choose healthier foods, and try to get more rest,
Take control of my mind and put it to the test.

I cannot let the world defeat me, I am stronger than that,
I'll surround myself with positivity, wear my mindset like a hat,
I'll take deep breaths and let go of the things I can't control,
Only then will I find peace, and the anxiety dispel.

So, let's take it one day at a time, I'll learn to love myself again,
Bring a little sunshine into my life, and let it begin,
It's time to put my unhelpful habits in the past,
And open my arms to a future that looks bright at last.

30. A small talk

It starts with a hello, a simple greeting,
A smile on your face, a heart that's beating,
A nod of the head, a gesture of care,
A small talk that shows that you're willing to share.

Sometimes all it takes is just a few words,
To show a little kindness, to make someone feel heard,
A genuine interest in what they have to say,
A little empathy that helps them through their day.

For small talk can fix a lot of things,
It can bring people together with the hope it brings,
It can heal broken hearts and ease troubled minds,
It can bring a little light to someone who's blind.

So never underestimate the power of small talk,
The bridges it builds, the doors that unlock,
It's a simple thing, yet it can mean so much,
To show someone that you care with just a gentle touch.

So, let's take the time to connect, with the people around us,
To show them we're here, in a world that can cause us to fuss,
Let's lift each other up, with the words we say,
For small talk can fix a lot and make all the difference today.

31. A red flag

Caught up in his beauty, swept away by his charm,
I fell for his words; I was clueless and unarmed.
He was a red flag waving right in front of my face,
But I was blinded by love, caught up in his embrace.

I see it now, as clear as day,
He was a master manipulator, playing games to sway,
My heart and soul, he controlled with ease,
I was a puppet, dancing to his breeze.

But he was a red flag, waving threateningly in the wind.
I was blind, couldn't see the danger that was within.
I was Dora, exploring uncharted territory,
Lost in a world of emotions, it was a great story.

But the ending was bittersweet, tears were shed,
For I found myself in a labyrinth of dread.
The red flag was a warning, a sign of things to come,
He was not the one, I needed to run, needed to be done.

Now I am wiser, better prepared for love's journey,
I won't be fooled again, by passion's sweet symphony.
I'll embrace the red flags, and heed their warning call,
For love is not blind, it's a choice, a conscious freefall.

32. The sorrow can help

On the things that matter, on the blessings we often overlook
The moments that slip by, unnoticed, until we're shook.
By the sting of heartbreak and the ache of loss
We're reminded of the value of what we've got, no matter the cost.

And so, we learn to be grateful, to cherish every day.
To find joy in the small things, to appreciate the sun's rays.
To love fiercely and forgive freely, to let go of bitterness.
To hold tight to the memories, the moments of tenderness

For it's in the midst of sorrow that we find our strength
We rise from the ashes; we go to any length.
To rebuild and to heal, to start anew with hope.
For in the darkest moments, it's our resilience that helps us cope.

So, let us not fear pain, but embrace it as a friend.
For it teaches us to grow, to love, to transcend.
Our limitations and fears, to live life to its fullest.
To never forget that in every moment, we are blessed and beautiful.

33. A dreamer

There once was a dreamer so bold,
Who dared to reach for the sky,
With a heart full of wonder and soul so old,
She aimed to reach the highest high.

She climbed to the mountaintops,
And soared through the clouds so white,
She pushed through the limits and the stops,
And gazed at the world in sight.

Through the trials and the testings,
She never let go of her will,
Through the falls and the blessings,
Her passion kept burning still.

And though the obstacles were many,
And the journey was long and hard,
She kept striding through each alley,
With a heart that refused to be marred.

And in the end when she had reached,
The goal she had longed to attain,
She looked back and smiled and preached,
"Belief is where victory begins its reign."

For anything in the world can be achieved,
If only you dare to dream and believe.

ABOUT THE AUTHOR

Ayn is just a student with great hopes and creative dreams. Raised on an unhealthy dose of optimism and fantasy fiction by her mother she has her own library of 172 books. She is a lover of naps, reads anything and loves writing. In her pastime she loves to play basketball and read novels. One of her biggest motivations to write poems was her teacher who loved to listen to her thoughts in the form of poetry.

Writer's Pocket

Writer's Pocket is a publication house established in 2016. We began with the aim of providing a better publishing platform for aspiring writers and budding poets.

The publishing industry in India (and around the world, to a great extent) is always something of a mystery even to the writers themselves. We are working on making publishing more accessible to everyone.

So far, we have helped over 3,000 writers turn their dreams into reality by publishing the books and continue to do so. By doing so, we also provide some of the best content by Indian writers to the readers.

Want to read more books? Scan this QR code with your smartphone and check out all our books on Amazon.